Mini-Mini Musicals

Written by
Jean Warren

Illustrated by Marion Hopping Ekberg
and
Paula Inmon

Warren Publishing House, Inc.
P.O. Box 2255, Everett, WA 98203

Editor: Elizabeth S. McKinnon
Production Editors: Brenda Mann Harrison
                     Gayle Bittinger
Cover Design: Larry Countryman

ISBN 0-911019-14-6

Library of Congress Catalog Card Number 86-051508
Printed in the United States of America
Distributed by: Gryphon House, Inc.
          P.O. Box 275
          Mt. Rainier, MD 20712

Contents

Introduction

Welcome to the fun of Mini-Mini Musicals — creative dramatics with music written especially for young children!

Although these musicals are presented as stage productions, they also can be used as part of story time or music time or as starting points for other learning activities. Outlined below are five steps that can be followed when working with any of the musicals.

Step One: Select a musical and use it at story time. Sing and tell the story to the children. Encourage them to sing parts of the songs. Repeat this activity for several days until the children are familiar with the songs and the storyline.

Step Two: Turn your story time or music time into creative movement time. Let the children decide how the characters in the musical should act as they (or you) sing the songs. Let all the children dramatize all of the parts. (In most cases, this may be as far as you want to go with the musical. If desired, you could extend the story theme by presenting related art, science and other learning activities.)

Step Three: If the children are enthusiastic about the musical, let them each choose a character group to join. Have them act out their parts while everyone who wants to sings along.

Step Four: If interest is still high, turn the musical into a problem-solving activity by letting the children help plan and make simple props. (Prop suggestions can be found at the end of each musical as well as in the section that begins on p. 67.) Then let the children sing and act out the musical using their new props.

Step Five: Use the musical when you need to put on a performance in front of an audience. By now the children will be performing material that is familiar to them. They will feel confident because they will be performing in groups rather than individually. And, most importantly, they will be having a good time!

Finally, please feel free to change or to adapt the musicals in any way you wish to suit the needs of your children. Enjoy!

Jean Warren

Teddy Bears' Picnic

CHARACTERS: Narrator (Adult)   Teddy Bears

(Teddy Bears are onstage in their house, fast asleep.)

NARRATOR: Wake up, everyone! Today's the day the teddy bears have their picnic.

(Teddy Bears wake up, stretch and yawn.)

TEDDY BEARS: **TODAY IS THE DAY**
Sung to: "The Battle Hymn of the Republic"

Today is the day that the teddy bears will play,
Today is the day that the teddy bears will play,
Today is the day that the teddy bears will play.
Hurray, hurray, hurray!

Time to get up and comb our fuzzy hair,
Time to get up and eat our breakfast fare,
Time to get ready, for this is our special day.
Hurray, hurray, hurray!

(Teddy Bears form into two groups. The Teddy Bears in the First Group step forward and pretend to look in a mirror while facing the audience.)

FIRST GROUP:

I'M A POOR LITTLE BEAR
Sung to: "Little White Duck"

I'm a poor little bear with nothing to wear.
A poor little bear, it really is unfair.
I have a new suit, but it has a tear.
Now I've nothing but my underwear.
I'm a poor little bear, now everyone will stare.
Boo, hoo, hoo!

SECOND GROUP:

YOU SILLY LITTLE BEAR
Sung to: "Little White Duck"

You silly little bear, no one will stare.
You silly little bear, no one will care.
A bear is not supposed to wear
Clothes all over its fuzzy hair.
You're a silly little bear, we all declare.
Silly, silly, silly!

NARRATOR:

Everybody ready? Let's go!

(Teddy Bears gather up picnic basket and blanket and walk offstage in pairs.)

TEDDY BEARS:

TEDDY BEARS' PICNIC
Sung to: "The Teddy Bears' Picnic"

Let's all go to the woods today,
We're sure of a big surprise.
Let's all go to the woods today,
We'll walk there side by side.
We know that we'll have lots of fun,
We'll eat and play and dance and run.
Today's the day the teddy bears have their picnic.

(Narrator places honey tree prop in center of stage. Teddy Bears turn around and walk back onstage in pairs into the woods.)

NARRATOR: Look, everyone! A honey tree!

TEDDY BEARS: Here we are at the woods today,
Here is our big surprise.
Here we are at the woods today,
We walked here side by side.
Now we'll all have lots of fun,
We'll eat and play and dance and run.
Today's the day the teddy bears have their picnic.

(Teddy Bears put blanket and picnic basket down at side of stage.)

NARRATOR: Let's walk around the tree and help ourselves to some honey!

(Teddy Bears walk in a circle around honey tree.)

TEDDY BEARS: **HERE WE GO ROUND THE HONEY TREE**
Sung to: "The Mulberry Bush"

Here we go round the honey tree,
Honey tree, honey tree.
Here we go round the honey tree,
So early in the morning.

Let's all reach and have a taste,
Have a taste, have a taste.
Let's all reach and have a taste,
So early in the morning.

(Teddy Bears form in pairs and skip around tree.)

TEDDY BEARS: **BEES IN MY HONEY**
Sung to: "Skip to My Lou"

Bees in my honey, shoo, shoo, shoo,
Bees in my honey, shoo, shoo, shoo,
Bees in my honey, shoo, shoo, shoo.
Skip round the tree of honey.

Ants in my honey, shoo, shoo, shoo,
Ants in my honey, shoo, shoo, shoo,
Ants in my honey, shoo, shoo, shoo.
Skip round the tree of honey.

Bears in a circle, two by two,
Bears in a circle, two by two,
Bears in a circle, two by two.
Skip round the tree of honey.

NARRATOR: Time to eat!

(Narrator removes tree prop while Teddy Bears move blanket and picnic basket to center of stage. They sit down, pass the picnic basket and begin to eat.)

TEDDY BEARS: **IT'S TIME**
Sung to: "The Farmer in the Dell"

It's time to eat our lunch,
It's time to eat our lunch.
Heigh-ho the derry-oh,
It's time to eat our lunch.

(Teddy Bears pack up picnic things.)

It's time to clean up,
It's time to clean up.
Heigh-ho the derry-oh,
It's time to clean up.

(Teddy Bears line up in pairs.)

It's time to head on home,
It's time to head on home.
Heigh-ho the derry-oh,
It's time to head on home.

(Teddy Bears march offstage carrying blanket and picnic basket.)

TEDDY BEARS: **WHEN THE BEARS GO MARCHING HOME**
Sung to: "When the Saints Go Marching In"

Oh, when the bears go marching home,
Oh, when the bears go marching home,
We will all march together,
When the bears go marching home.

(Teddy Bears turn around and walk back onstage into their house.)

TEDDY BEARS:

TEDDY BEARS' PICNIC
Sung to: "The Teddy Bears' Picnic"

We went down to the woods today,
We had our big surprise.
We went down to the woods today,
We went there side by side.
We ate and played and ran and danced,
We skipped and rolled and leaped and pranced.
Today's the day the teddy bears had their picnic.

THE END

Suggested Props: A blanket; a basket; a decorated chair or other object to use as a honey tree. Additional prop and costume suggestions for this musical can be found on p. 68.

Down Storybook Lane

CHARACTERS:	Narrator (Adult) Three Bears Children Three Blind Mice Three Little Pigs Three Little Kittens

(Children walk onstage.)

NARRATOR: Here come the children down Storybook Lane!

(Children continue walking around stage.)

CHILDREN:

DOWN STORYBOOK LANE
Sung to: "The Muffin Man"

Let's go walking down the lane,
Down the lane, down the lane.
Let's go walking down the lane,
Down Storybook Lane.

We will meet our storybook friends,
Our storybook friends, our storybook friends.
We will meet our storybook friends
Who live down Storybook Lane.

(Three Little Pigs walk onstage.)

Here come the Three Little Pigs,
The Three Little Pigs, the Three Little Pigs.
Here come the Three Little Pigs
Who live down Storybook Lane.

(Three Bears walk onstage.)

Here come the Three Bears,
The Three Bears, the Three Bears.
Here come the Three Bears
Who live down Storybook Lane.

(Three Blind Mice walk onstage.)

Here come the Three Blind Mice,
The Three Blind Mice, the Three Blind Mice.
Here come the Three Blind Mice
Who live down Storybook Lane.

(Three Little Kittens walk onstage.)

Here come the Three Little Kittens,
The Three Little Kittens, the Three Little Kittens.
Here come the Three Little Kittens
Who live down Storybook Lane.

*(Children move to back of stage. Each group of three
Storybook Characters faces audience and holds hands.)*

**STORYBOOK
CHARACTERS:**

ONE, TWO, THREE
Sung to: "Three Blind Mice"

One, two, three. One, two, three.
As you see, we're all three.

*(Each group of Storybook Characters joins hands in a circle
and skips around.)*

Whenever we go out to play,
We always seem to stay this way.
We're together night and day.
One, two, three.

*(All Characters walk offstage. Three Little Pigs run back
onstage and begin to hammer and build.)*

THREE LITTLE PIGS: **WE'RE THREE LITTLE PIGS**
Sung to: "Little White Duck"

We're Three Little Pigs, always in a hurry,
Building our homes so we don't have to worry.
We work all day from morn to night,
Making our homes so they're wolf-proof tight.
Oh, we're Three Little Pigs, always in a hurry.
Work, work, work!

(Three Little Pigs run offstage. Three Bears walk onstage holding hands and swinging arms.)

THREE BEARS: **PAPA, MAMA, BABY BEAR**
Sung to: "London Bridge"

Papa, Mama, Baby Bear,
Baby Bear, Baby Bear.
Papa, Mama, Baby Bear.
We're the Three Bears.

We-e live in the woods,
In the woods, in the woods.
We-e live in the woods,
In our little house.

(Three Bears circle around stage.)

Once when we were out for a walk,
Out for a walk, out for a walk,
Once when we were out for a walk,
In came Goldilocks.

We wish she would have stayed and played,
Stayed and played, stayed and played.
We wish she would have stayed and played,
But she ran away.

Papa, Mama, Baby Bear,
Baby Bear, Baby Bear.
Papa, Mama, Baby Bear.
We're the Three Bears.

(Three Bears walk offstage. Three Blind Mice scurry onstage and chase around.)

THREE BLIND MICE: **THREE BLIND MICE**
Sung to: "Three Blind Mice"

We're Three Blind Mice, we're Three Blind Mice.
See how we run, see how we run.
We run all through the night and day,
We run when we go out to play,
We never stop, we never stay.
Run, run, run!

(Three Blind Mice scurry offstage. Three Little Kittens skip onstage holding up their hands.)

THREE LITTLE   **THREE LITTLE KITTENS**
KITTENS: **Sung to:** "Jack and Jill"

We're Three Little Kittens who've lost our mittens,
So now we have to cry.
Mother dear, see here, see here,
Our mittens we have lost.

NARRATOR: Lost your mittens? You naughty kittens!
Then you shall have no pie!

THREE LITTLE   Boo, hoo, hoo! Boo, hoo, hoo!
KITTENS: Now we shall have no pie.

(Three Little Kittens look around, then reach into their pockets and pull out mittens.)

We Three Little Kittens, we found our mittens.
Now we don't have to cry.
Mother dear, see here, see here,
Our mittens we have found.

NARRATOR: Found your mittens? You good little kittens!
Now you shall have your pie.

THREE LITTLE   Yum, yum, yum! Oh, what fun!
KITTENS: Now we'll wave goodbye.

(Three Little Kittens wave and skip offstage. Children walk onstage and face audience.)

CHILDREN:

DOWN STORYBOOK LANE
Sung to: "The Muffin Man"

Now you've met our storybook friends,
Our storybook friends, our storybook friends.
Now you've met our storybook friends
Who live down Storybook Lane.

(Storybook Characters walk onstage single file and shake hands with Children. Children repeat following verse until all Storybook Characters are onstage.)

We will greet them once again,
Once again, once again.
We will greet them once again
Here on Storybook Lane.

(All Characters face audience and bow, then walk offstage.)

ALL CHARACTERS:

Now we must be on our way,
On our way, on our way.
Now we must be on our way,
Back down Storybook Lane.

THE END

Suggested Props: Mittens for Three Little Kittens. Additional prop and costume suggestions for this musical can be found on p. 69.

Off to Bed We Go

CHARACTERS: Narrator (Adult)   Midnight Monsters
Children   Stars
Shadows

NARRATOR: It's time for bed, children!

*(All Characters enter and march around stage. Shadows,
Midnight Monsters and Stars also act as Children.)*

CHILDREN: **OFF TO BED WE GO**
Sung to: "The Farmer in the Dell"

Oh, off to bed we go,
Off to bed we go.
Heigh-ho the derry-oh,
Off to bed we go.

Let's sing as we go,
Let's sing as we go.
Heigh-ho the derry-oh,
Let's sing as we go.

We're not afraid to go,
We're not afraid to go.
Heigh-ho the derry-oh,
We're not afraid to go.

(Children hop into bed on floor.)

First we'll jump in bed,
Then lay down our heads.
Heigh-ho the derry-oh,
We'll lay down our heads.

We'll cover up real tight,
Then turn out the light.

(Narrator turns off lights.)

Heigh-ho the derry-oh,
We'll turn out the light.

(Shadows sneak out of bed and go behind sheet hung across back of stage.)

It's pretty dark in here,
We've nothing to fear.
Heigh-ho the derry-oh,
We've nothing to fear.

Did you hear a sound?
We better check around.
Heigh-ho the derry-oh,
We better check around.

(Narrator turns on bright light behind sheet. Shadows dance around between sheet and bright light.)

NARRATOR: There's nothing to fear, children. It's just shadows dancing on the wall.

(Shadows stop dancing. Children get out of bed and stand up.)

CHILDREN: **I SEE SHADOWS**
Sung to: "Skip to My Lou"

I see shadows on the wall,
I see shadows on the wall,
I see shadows on the wall.
Some are big and some are small.

Watch them move like I do,
    (Children and Shadows raise hands.)
Watch them move like I do,
    (Children and Shadows lower hands.)
Watch them move like I do.
    (Children and Shadows crouch down low.)
I pop up and they do, too!
    (Children and Shadows jump up.)

Back to bed we must go,
Back to bed we must go,
Back to bed we must go.
Who's afraid of a shadow!

(Children get back into bed. Narrator turns off bright light behind sheet. Shadows come out from behind sheet and lie down in bed with other Children. Midnight Monsters sneak out of bed and go offstage.)

CHILDREN:

MIDNIGHT MONSTERS
Sung to: "My Bonnie Lies Over the Ocean"

Sometimes when we go to bed
And try to fall asleep,
We know that big hairy monsters
Into our room do creep.

(Midnight Monsters creep back onstage.)

Creep, creep, creep, creep,
Yes, into our room they creep.
Creep, creep, creep, creep,
Yes, into our room they creep.

We cover our eyes when they come,
But sometimes we chance a peek.
Those silly old monsters are dancing,
Across the room they leap.

(Midnight Monsters leap around stage.)

Leap, leap, leap, leap,
Across the room they leap.
Leap, leap, leap, leap,
Across the room they leap.

We really must go to sleep now,
It's getting so late at night.
The only way to scare monsters
Is to turn back on the light.

(Narrator turns on lights. Midnight Monsters run offstage.)

Turn, turn, turn, turn,
We'll turn back on the light.
Turn, turn, turn, turn,
We'll turn back on the light.

The monsters all are gone now,
We really must get some sleep.
We'll turn off the light now
And not make another peep.

(Narrator turns off lights.)

Peep, peep, peep, peep,
We'll not make another peep.
Peep, peep, peep, peep,
We'll not make another peep.

(Midnight Monsters creep back onstage and lie down in bed with other Children. Stars sneak out of bed, tiptoe to back of stage and blink small flashlights on and off.)

NARRATOR: Look, children, the stars are shining through the window! Let's make wishes!

(Children sit up in bed and look toward Stars.)

CHILDREN: **TWINKLE, TWINKLE, LITTLE STARS**
Sung to: "Music, Music, Music"

Twinkle, twinkle, little stars,
Friends of Jupiter and Mars,
All you do the whole night through
Is twinkle, twinkle, twinkle.
Shine, oh, friends of mine.
If wishes really, really do come true,
I will wish tonight on you.
Please, oh please, oh please come true,
The wish I wish tonight on you,
Then tomorrow all day through
I'll twinkle, twinkle, twinkle.

Twinkle, twinkle, little stars,
Friends of Jupiter and Mars,
All you do the whole night through
Is twinkle, twinkle, twinkle.
Shine, oh, friends of mine.
If wishes really, really do come true,
I will wish tonight on you.
Now it's back to sleep we go,
Dreaming 'bout the stars that glow,
Dreaming 'bout our wishes, too,
Good night, good night to you.

CHILDREN: Good night!

(Children lie back down in bed and go to sleep.)

THE END

Suggested Props: A sheet; a bright light to place behind sheet; small flashlights for Stars. Additional prop and costume suggestions for this musical can be found on p. 70.

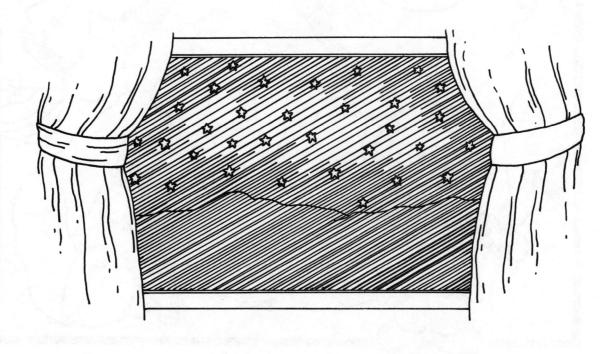

23

Santa's Workshop

CHARACTERS:

Narrator (Adult)	Trains
Elves	Toy Soldiers
Dancing Dolls	Tops

(Dancing Dolls, Trains, Toy Soldiers and Tops are lined up onstage.)

NARRATOR: Far up at the North Pole, the elves are busy making Christmas toys.

(Elves walk onstage and begin working on Toys.)

ELVES: **THIS IS THE WAY WE MAKE THE TOYS**
Sung to: "The Mulberry Bush"

This is the way we hammer the toys,
Hammer the toys, hammer the toys.
This is the way we hammer the toys
We make for Christmas morning.

This is the way we sew the toys,
Sew the toys, sew the toys.
This is the way we sew the toys
We make for Christmas morning.

This is the way we paint the toys,
Paint the toys, paint the toys.
This is the way we paint the toys
We make for Christmas morning.

NARRATOR: At last all the toys are finished. Now the elves must check them to see if they work. First they will wind up the dancing dolls.

(Elves walk over to Dancing Dolls and wind them up. Elves step back while Dancing Dolls move forward and begin dancing around.)

DANCING DOLLS: **I AM DANCING**
Sung to: "Frere Jacques"

I am dancing, I am dancing,
Round and round, round and round.
First I dance one way,
Then I dance the other way.
Round and round, round and round.

I am dancing, I am dancing,
Round and round, round and round.
First I dance one way,
Then I dance the other way.
Now sit down, now sit down.

(Dancing Dolls sit down.)

NARRATOR: Next, the elves will wind up the trains.

(Elves walk over to Trains and wind them up. Elves step back while Trains move forward and begin chugging around.)

TRAINS: **I AM CHUGGING**
Sung to: "Frere Jacques"

I am chugging, I am chugging,
Round and round, round and round.
First I chug one way,
Then I chug the other way.
Round and round, round and round.

I am chugging, I am chugging,
Round and round, round and round.
First I chug one way,
Then I chug the other way.
Now sit down, now sit down.

(Trains sit down.)

NARRATOR:

Now the elves will wind up the toy soldiers.

(Elves walk over to Toy Soldiers and wind them up. Elves step back while Toy Soldiers move forward and begin marching around.)

TOY SOLDIERS:

I AM MARCHING
Sung to: "Frere Jacques"

I am marching, I am marching,
Round and round, round and round.
First I march one way,
Then I march the other way.
Round and round, round and round.

I am marching, I am marching,
Round and round, round and round.
First I march one way,
Then I march the other way.
Now sit down, now sit down.

(Toy Soldiers sit down.)

NARRATOR:

Now the elves will wind up the tops.

(Elves walk over to Tops and wind them up. Elves step back while Tops move forward and begin twirling around.)

TOPS: **I AM SPINNING**
                           Sung to: "Frere Jacques"

                           I am spinning, I am spinning,
                           Round and round, round and round.
                           First I spin one way,
                           Then I spin the other way.
                           Round and round, round and round.

                           I am spinning, I am spinning,
                           Round and round, round and round.
                           First I spin one way,
                           Then I spin the other way.
                           Now sit down, now sit down.

                           (Tops sit down.)

NARRATOR: The elves have finished checking all the toys. Now they
                           will wrap them up.

                           *(All Toys stand while Elves circle around them, moving
                           them to center of stage. Then Elves wrap up Toys.)*

ELVES: **YOU ARE READY**
                           Sung to: "Frere Jacques"

                           You are ready, you are ready
                           For Santa's sleigh, for Santa's sleigh.
                           We wrapped you up and packed you up,
                           We tied you up and sacked you up
                           For Christmas Day, for Christmas Day.

                           *(Elves walk offstage. All Toys stand together as if riding on
                           Santa's sleigh.)*

ALL TOYS:

ON SANTA'S SLEIGH
Sung to: "Jingle Bells"

Here we are today,
All on Santa's sleigh.
Oh, what fun we'll have
When it's Christmas Day.
We'll dance around and sing,
We'll clap and jump for joy,
When we see those great big smiles
On every girl and boy, oh —

Jingle bells, jingle bells,
Jingle all the way.
Oh, what fun it is to ride
On Santa's Christmas sleigh.
Jingle bells, jingle bells,
Jingle all the way.
Oh, what fun it is to ride
On Santa's Christmas sleigh!

THE END

Suggested Props: Prop and costume suggestions for this musical can be found on p.71.

Singing in the Rain

CHARACTERS:

Narrator (Adult)   Pigs
Children   Ducks
Farmers

(Children are onstage in their house looking bored and unhappy.)

NARRATOR: Oh, what a boring day! It's raining outside.

(Children sing next two songs in a slow, singsong manner.)

CHILDREN: **OH, WHAT A BORING MORNING**
Sung to: "Oh, What a Beautiful Morning"

Oh, what a boring morning,
Oh, what a boring day.
It is raining outside,
So we cannot play.

CHILDREN: **RAIN, RAIN, GO AWAY**
Sung to: "Skip to My Lou"

Rain, rain, go away,
Rain, rain, go away.
Rain, rain, go away,
So we can go out and play.

CHILDREN:

RAIN, RAIN, RAIN
Sung to: "Music, Music, Music"

When we look into the skies,
We get raindrops in our eyes.
All it does the whole day through
Is rain, rain, rain.
Rain is such a pain.
It makes you stay inside the whole day through
With nothing fun at all to do.
We just wish that we could play
And the rain would go away.
But all it ever seems to do
Is rain, rain, rain.

NARRATOR:

Come on, everyone, let's go outside! Maybe we can find something to do.

(Children put on raingear and walk offstage. Then they turn around and walk back onstage into the outdoors.)

NARRATOR:

Oh, look! Here come some happy farmers!

(Farmers walk onstage.)

CHILDREN:

THE FARMERS FROM THE DELL
Sung to: "The Farmer in the Dell"

It's the farmers from the dell,
The farmers from the dell.
Heigh-ho the derry-oh,
It's the farmers from the dell.

Why do you look so well?
Why do you look so well?
Heigh-ho the derry-oh,
Why do you look so well?

FARMERS:

Oh, can't you tell?
Oh, can't you tell?
Heigh-ho the derry-oh,
Oh, can't you tell?

32

Because the rain fell,
Because the rain fell.
Heigh-ho the derry-oh,
Because the rain fell.

Our crops will grow so well,
Our crops will grow so well.
Heigh-ho the derry-oh,
Our crops will grow so well.

CHILDREN:

Gee, that is swell,
Gee, that is swell.
Heigh-ho the derry-oh,
Your crops will grow so well.

(Farmers walk offstage.)

NARRATOR:

Here come some pigs! It sure looks like they enjoy the rain!

(Pigs skip onstage.)

PIGS:

DOWN ON THE FARM
Sung to: "Up on the Housetop"

Down on the farm we love to play
In the mud all through the day.
That is why we love to spy
Great big rain clouds in the sky.
Rain, rain, rain, we love you.
Rain, rain, rain, yes, we do.
Great big rain clouds in the sky,
Please, oh please, don't pass us by.

Down in the mud we make a hole,
Where we like to roll and roll.
That is why we shout "Hurray!"
Every time it rains today.
Rain, rain, rain, we love you.
Rain, rain, rain, yes, we do.
Great big rain clouds in the sky,
Please, oh please, don't pass us by.

(Pigs skip offstage.)

NARRATOR:

Here come some smiling ducks!

(Ducks waddle onstage.)

DUCKS:

WE'RE LITTLE YELLOW DUCKS
Sung to: "Little White Duck"

We're little yellow ducks
Who love to see the rain.
Little yellow ducks,
Now we will explain.
We love to see the rain come down,
Making puddles all over town.
Oh, we're little yellow ducks
Who love to see the rain.
Splish, splish, splash!

We're little yellow ducks
Who love to swim and splash.
We wish the rain
Would last and last and last.
We love to see the rain come down,
Then we can swim all over town.
Oh, we're little yellow ducks
Who love to see the rain.
Splish, splish, splash!

(Ducks waddle offstage.)

NARRATOR:

Gee, I guess the rain really helps everyone. Maybe the rain isn't so bad after all!

CHILDREN:

IT IS RAINING EVERYWHERE
Sung to: "The Good Ship Lollipop"

It is raining everywhere,
It is raining, and we don't care.
Come on, let's play
While we watch the rain today.

It is raining on the hills,
It is raining on the daffodils.
Come on, let's play
While we watch the rain today.

It is raining on treetops,
It is raining on farmers' crops.
Come on, let's play
While we watch the rain today.

It is raining on the pond,
And the ducks keep swimming on.
Come on, let's play
While we watch the rain today.

34

(Farmers, Pigs and Ducks walk back onstage.)

ALL CHARACTERS: **WE'RE SINGING IN THE RAIN**
Sung to: "Singing in the Rain"

We're singing in the rain,
Just singing in the rain.
Those clouds up above
Bring the rain that we love.
We shout "Hip, hurray!"
We're happy today,
Just singing, singing in the rain.

Let the stormy clouds chase
Other folks from this place.
Let the rain fall and fall,
We don't mind it at all.
We skip and we prance,
We laugh and we dance,
Just singing, singing in the rain.

THE END

Suggested Props: Prop and costume suggestions for this musical can be found on p. 72.

Dancing Colors

CHARACTERS: Narrator (Adult)   Green
                    Children   Yellow
                    Purple   Orange
                    Blue   Red

(Children are lined up at back of stage.)

NARRATOR: Look, children! The colors are dancing into town!

                    (Groups of Purple, Blue, Green, Yellow, Orange and Red dance onstage.)

CHILDREN: **THE COLORS ARE DANCING INTO TOWN**
                    Sung to: "When Johnny Comes Marching Home"

                    The colors are dancing into town, hurray, hurray!
                    The colors are dancing into town, we hope they stay.
                    The colors dance in, there's purple and blue,
                    Green, yellow, orange and red, too.
                    Oh, we're all so glad, we hope they want to stay.

                    The colors are dancing all around, hurray, hurray!
                    The colors are dancing all around, we hope they stay.
                    The colors are dancing here and there,
                    The colors are dancing everywhere.
                    Oh, we're all so glad, we hope they want to stay.

                    The colors are making everything so bright today,
                    The colors are making everything so bright and gay.
                    The colors dance in, there's purple and blue,
                    Green, yellow, orange and red, too.
                    Oh, we're all so glad, we hope they want to stay.

(Colors dance to back of stage. Purple steps forward and begins dancing and placing purple objects around stage. Other Colors sing along with Children.)

CHILDREN:

PURPLE IS DANCING ALL AROUND
Sung to: "When Johnny Comes Marching Home"

Purple is dancing all around, hurray, hurray!
Purple is dancing all around, we hope it stays.
Eggplants, grapes and violets, too,
Purple, we love you! Yes, we do!
And we're all so glad that purple is here today.

(Purple dances to back of stage. Blue steps forward and begins dancing and placing blue objects around stage. Other Colors sing along with Children.)

CHILDREN:

BLUE IS DANCING ALL AROUND
Sung to: "When Johnny Comes Marching Home"

Blue is dancing all around, hurray, hurray!
Blue is dancing all around, we hope it stays.
Sky and lakes and bluebirds, too,
Blue, we love you! Yes, we do!
And we're all so glad that blue is here today.

(Blue dances to back of stage. Green steps forward and begins dancing and placing green objects around stage. Other Colors sing along with Children.)

CHILDREN:

GREEN IS DANCING ALL AROUND
Sung to: "When Johnny Comes Marching Home"

Green is dancing all around, hurray, hurray!
Green is dancing all around, we hope it stays.
Grass and trees and lettuce, too,
Green, we love you! Yes, we do!
And we're all so glad that green is here today.

(Green dances to back of stage. Yellow steps forward and begins dancing and placing yellow objects around stage. Other Colors sing along with Children.)

CHILDREN:

YELLOW IS DANCING ALL AROUND
Sung to: "When Johnny Comes Marching Home"

Yellow is dancing all around, hurray, hurray!
Yellow is dancing all around, we hope it stays.
Bananas, sun and lemons, too,
Yellow, we love you! Yes, we do!
And we're all so glad that yellow is here today.

(Yellow dances to back of stage. Orange steps forward and begins dancing and placing orange objects around stage. Other Colors sing along with Children.)

CHILDREN:

ORANGE IS DANCING ALL AROUND
Sung to: "When Johnny Comes Marching Home"

Orange is dancing all around, hurray, hurray!
Orange is dancing all around, we hope it stays.
Pumpkins, juice and carrots, too,
Orange, we love you! Yes, we do!
And we're all so glad that orange is here today.

(Orange dances to back of stage. Red steps forward and begins dancing and placing red objects around stage. Other Colors sing along with Children.)

CHILDREN:

RED IS DANCING ALL AROUND
Sung to: "When Johnny Comes Marching Home"

Red is dancing all around, hurray, hurray!
Red is dancing all around, we hope it stays.
Apples, berries, cherries, too,
Red, we love you! Yes, we do!
And we're all so glad that red is here today.

(Other Colors step forward and join Red in dancing around stage.)

CHILDREN:

THE COLORS ARE DANCING ALL AROUND
Sung to: "When Johnny Comes Marching Home"

The colors are dancing all around the town today,
The colors are dancing all around, we hope they stay.
First they're low and then they're high,
Now they're dancing in the sky.
And we're all so glad the colors came to stay.

(Colors line up as if forming a rainbow, with Purple at the "bottom" and Red at the "top.")

NARRATOR: Oh, look! The colors have made a rainbow!

ALL CHARACTERS:

RAINBOW COLORS
Sung to: "Hush, Little Baby"

Rainbow purple, rainbow blue,
Rainbow green and yellow, too.
Rainbow orange, rainbow red,
Rainbow smiling overhead.

Come and count the colors with me.
How many colors can you see?
One, two, three, up to green,
Four, five, six colors can be seen.

Rainbow purple, rainbow blue,
Rainbow green and yellow, too.
Rainbow orange, rainbow red,
Rainbow smiling overhead.

THE END

Prop Suggestions: Colored construction paper headbands for Colors; colored objects or paper cutouts for Colors to place around stage. Additional prop and costume suggestions for this musical can be found on p. 73.

40

In a Spring Garden

CHARACTERS: Flowers   Bees
                         Birds   Butterflies

(Flowers walk onstage and stand in a row.)

ALL CHARACTERS: **OUT IN THE GARDEN**
                         Sung to: "Down by the Station"

                         Out in the garden in the month of May,
                         See the pretty flowers standing in a row.

                         (Birds fly onstage.)

                         See the little birds flying down to greet them.
                         Tweet, tweet, tweet, tweet, off they go.

                         (Birds fly to back of stage.)

                         Out in the garden in the month of May,
                         See the pretty flowers standing in a row.

                         (Bees fly onstage.)

                         See the little bees flying down to greet them.
                         Buzz, buzz, buzz, buzz, off they go.

                         (Bees fly to back of stage.)

Out in the garden in the month of May,
See the pretty flowers standing in a row.

(Butterflies fly onstage.)

See the little butterflies flying down to greet them.
Flit, flit, flit, flit, off they go.

(Butterflies fly to back of stage. Then Birds, Bees and Butterflies step forward in line with Flowers. All Characters join hands and walk around in a circle.)

ALL CHARACTERS: **IN OUR SPRINGTIME GARDEN**
Sung to: "The Mulberry Bush"

What a lovely time of year,
Time of year, time of year.
What a lovely time of year
In our springtime garden.

(All Characters kneel, except Flowers, who sway back and forth.)

See the flowers swing and sway,
Swing and sway, swing and sway.
See the flowers swing and sway
In our springtime garden.

(All Characters stand up, join hands and walk around in a circle.)

What a lovely time of year,
Time of year, time of year.
What a lovely time of year
In our springtime garden.

(All Characters kneel, except Birds, who flap their wings and chirp.)

Hear the birds chirp all day,
Chirp all day, chirp all day.
Hear the birds chirp all day
In our springtime garden.

(All Characters stand up, join hands and walk around in a circle.)

What a lovely time of year,
Time of year, time of year.
What a lovely time of year
In our springtime garden.

(All Characters kneel, except Bees, who buzz around.)

Hear the bees buzz and play,
Buzz and play, buzz and play.
Hear the bees buzz and play
In our springtime garden.

(All Characters stand up, join hands and walk around in a circle.)

What a lovely time of year,
Time of year, time of year.
What a lovely time of year
In our springtime garden.

(All Characters kneel, except Butterflies, who wave their wings.)

See the butterflies today,
Here today, here today.
See the butterflies today
In our springtime garden.

(All Characters stand up, join hands and walk around in a circle.)

Let's all circle round and sing,
Round and sing, round and sing.
Let's all circle round and sing
In our springtime garden.

(Flowers stand in a row while Birds, Bees and Butterflies fly around stage.)

ALL CHARACTERS:

IT'S SPRING
Sung to: "Music, Music, Music"

Let's all sing our song today,
Let's all sing because it's May.
Let's all sing in our own way,
It's spring, it's spring, it's spring!
Spring, a time to sing,
A time to say hello to everyone
And join in the garden fun.
Let's all sing our song today,
Let's all sing because it's May.
Let's all sing in our own way,
It's spring, it's spring, it's spring!

THE END

Suggested Prop: Prop and costume suggestions for this musical can be found on p. 74.

Under the Big Top

CHARACTERS: Narrator (Adult)   Dancing Bears
                    Clowns   Elephants

(All Characters walk onstage.)

NARRATOR: Hurray, the circus has come to town! Let's watch them raise the circus tent!

(All Characters circle around stage, pulling on ropes as if raising tent.)

ALL CHARACTERS: **EVERYBODY CIRCLE ROUND**
Sung to: "Twinkle, Twinkle, Little Star"

Everybody circle round,
Lift the canvas off the ground.
Pull and pull and watch it rise,
Big Top grows before our eyes.
Everybody circle round,
Lift the canvas off the ground.

(All Characters form in a large circle to make a circus ring.)

Everybody circle round,
Form a ring upon the ground.
Now we're set to watch the show,
Circus acts both high and low.
Everybody circle round,
Form a ring upon the ground.

(All Characters sit down in place.)

NARRATOR: Ladies and gentlemen, welcome to the Big Top! The show is about to begin. Here come the clowns!

(Clowns stand up, move into center of ring and begin clowning around.)

ALL CHARACTERS: **FUNNY CLOWNS**
Sung to: "Frere Jacques"

Funny clowns, funny clowns,
Jump around, jump around.
Sometimes making faces,
Sometimes running races.
Funny clowns, funny clowns.

Funny clowns, funny clowns,
Spin around, spin around.
Sometimes with a big nose,
Sometimes with two big toes.
Funny clowns, funny clowns.

NARRATOR: Look, the clowns are going to make popcorn!

(Clowns crouch down and begin to hop and squirm.)

ALL CHARACTERS: **POP GO THE CLOWNS**
Sung to: "Pop Goes the Weasel"

See the funny popcorn clowns
Jumping in their pot.
Watch them while they squirm around.
Ouch! It's so hot!
See the kernels jump and squirm,
See them getting hotter.
Watch them while they all explode —
POP! goes the corn.

(Clowns jump up, pass out "popcorn" to Other Characters, then sit back down in ring.)

NARRATOR: Here come the dancing bears!

(Dancing Bears stand up, move into center of ring and begin to dance.)

ALL CHARACTERS: **HERE COME THE DANCING BEARS**
Sung to: "The Mulberry Bush"

Here come the dancing bears,
Dancing bears, dancing bears.
Here come the dancing bears,
All around the ring.

See them stand up on two legs,
On two legs, on two legs.
See them stand up on two legs,
All around the ring.

See them twirl around and around,
Around and around, around and around.
See them twirl around and around,
All around the ring.

See them jump and clap their hands,
Clap their hands, clap their hands.
See them jump and clap their hands,
All around the ring.

Goodbye, little dancing bears,
Dancing bears, dancing bears.
Goodbye, little dancing bears,
We like the way you dance.

(Dancing Bears sit back down in ring. Elephants stand up and form a line to one side of ring.)

NARRATOR: And now, ladies and gentlemen, we have the amazing elephant tightrope walkers, who will attempt to walk across the entire ring on a piece of string. Quiet, please!

(Narrator lays a long piece of string across middle of ring. One Elephant walks across string, turns around and walks back.)

ALL CHARACTERS: **ELEPHANTS BALANCING**
Sung to: "Mary Had a Little Lamb"

One little elephant balancing,
Balancing, balancing,
One little elephant balancing
On a piece of string.

(Elephant on string motions to another Elephant to walk out on string.)

(He/She) is having so much fun,
So much fun, so much fun,
(He/She) is having so much fun,
(He/She) calls a friend to come.

(The two Elephants on string walk across it, turn around and walk back.)

Two little elephants balancing,
Balancing, balancing,
Two little elephants balancing
On a piece of string.

(Elephants on string motion to another Elephant to walk out on string.)

They are having so much fun,
So much fun, so much fun,
They are having so much fun,
They call a friend to come.

(All Characters continue singing until last Elephant is motioned out onto string.)

(Five/Six/etc.) little elephants balancing,
Balancing, balancing,
(Five/Six/etc.) little elephants balancing
On a piece of string.

(Elephants walk off string and sit back down in ring. Narrator removes string.)

NARRATOR: Ladies and gentlemen, for our grand finale we invite you to feast your eyes on our Farewell Circus Parade!

(All Characters stand up and march around stage.)

ALL CHARACTERS: **FAREWELL CIRCUS SONG**
Sung to: "When the Saints Go Marching In"

Oh, it is time for us to go,
But we wanted you to know
That we all had a good time
At the circus here today.

Oh, we will march around once more,
Then we will march right out the door.
Oh, we wish that we could stay,
But we must be on our way.

ALL CHARACTERS: Goodbye!

(All Characters wave and march offstage.)

THE END

Suggested Props: A long piece of string to place across circus ring. Additional prop and costume suggestions for this musical can be found on p. 75.

In the Deep Blue Sea

CHARACTERS:

Narrator (Adult)	Crabs
Divers	Octopus
Fish	Oysters

(Divers are onstage by the sea. One by one, they jump into the water.)

NARRATOR:

Look! The divers are jumping into the deep blue sea!

(Divers swim around stage.)

DIVERS:

DOWN, DOWN, DOWN WE GO
Sung to: "Row, Row, Row Your Boat"

Down, down, down we go
To the bottom of the sea.
What will we find today?
What treasures will we see?

NARRATOR:

Here comes a school of fish!

(Fish swim onstage.)

FISH:

Glub, glub, glub, glub.
How are you today?
What kind of fish are you?
Can you stay and play?

DIVERS: Thank you, little fish,
                   We wish that we could stay.
                   But we are busy divers.
                   We have no time to play.

FISH: Goodbye, funny friends,
                   We wish that you could stay.
                   But if you have work to do,
                   We'll be on our way.

                   (Fish swim offstage while Divers continue swimming around.)

DIVERS: Down, down, down we go
                   To the bottom of the sea.
                   What will we find today?
                   What treasures will we see?

NARRATOR: Look! Here come some crabs!

                   (Crabs crawl sideways onstage.)

CRABS: **WE'RE LITTLE PINK CRABS**
                   Sung to: "Little White Duck"

                   We're little pink crabs
                   Who live down in the sea,
                   And wherever we go,
                   We're quick as we can be.
                   We always like to run and hide,
                   And when we walk, it's from side to side.
                   Oh, can you stay
                   And play awhile with us?
                   Please, please, please!

DIVERS: Hello, little crabs,
                   We're divers in the sea.
                   We came on down
                   To see what we could see.
                   We hope to find some treasure here.
                   Do you know of some treasure near?
                   Oh, we're busy little divers
                   With no time to play.
                   We're on our way.

                   (Crabs crawl offstage while Divers continue to swim around.)

NARRATOR: Here comes an octopus! Maybe she knows where to find some treasure.

(Four children walk onstage with their backs facing and their arms linked to make an Octopus. The children sit down and move their legs open and closed.)

OCTOPUS: **OH, WHAT A BEAUTIFUL MORNING**
Sung to: "Oh, What a Beautiful Morning"

Oh, what a beautiful morning,
Oh, what a beautiful day.
I love to swim in the ocean,
Moving my legs this way.

I love to play in the ocean,
I love to play in the bay.
But I haven't seen any treasure.
Can't you stay and play?

DIVERS: We'd love to play in the ocean,
We'd love to play in the bay.
But we must look for treasure,
So we'll be on our way.

(Divers continue swimming around stage. Fish, Crabs and Oysters swim onstage. Oysters sit down with knees pulled up to chests, arms crossed on knees and chins resting on arms. Each one hides a pearl prop in his or her lap.)

ALL SEA CREATURES: **WONDERS EVERYWHERE**
Sung to: "Up on the Housetop"

Here come the divers one by one,
Searching for treasure, that's no fun.
They should stop and look around,
Wonders everywhere could be found.
Shells, shells, shells, seaweed, too,
Lots of coral, pink and new.
Oh, how we wish that they would stay
To see the beauty here today.

ALL SEA CREATURES: **SHELLS, SHELLS, SHELLS**
Sung to: "Jingle Bells"

Giant shells, tiny shells,
Shells wherever you look.
There are so very many shells,
You could write a book.
Rainbow shells, purple shells,
Shells that curve around.
Can't they see the beauty here
Just lying on the ground?

NARRATOR: Come on, let's go play!

(All Sea Creatures, except Oysters, swim offstage. Divers swim over to Oysters.)

DIVERS: **HELLO, LITTLE OYSTERS**
Sung to: "Little White Duck"

Well hello, little oysters,
How are you today?
How come you
Did not go off to play?

OYSTERS: We wish that we could swim away,
But we're so heavy we cannot play.
We're poor little oysters
With rocks inside our shells.
Can you help?

DIVERS: Well now, little oysters,
We should be on our way,
But we will stop
And help you out today.
Open up your shells real wide,
And we'll take out what is heavy inside.

(Oysters raise heads and arms. Divers lean over Oysters and take out pearls.)

OYSTERS: Oh, we're happy little oysters
Who now can run and play.
Hip, hip, hurray!

(Oysters swim offstage. Divers face audience while holding up pearls.)

DIVERS:

ROCKS, ROCKS, ROCKS
Sung to: "Row, Row, Row Your Boat"

Rocks, rocks, rocks we've got,
Let's give our rocks a hurl.

(Divers start to throw away pearls, then stop and look at them carefully.)

Golly, gee, look and see,
Our rocks are really pearls!

THE END

Suggested Props: Ping-Pong balls or tennis balls to use as pearls for Oysters. Additional prop and costume suggestions for this musical can be found on p. 76.

Yankee Doodle Parade

CHARACTERS: Narrator (Adult)   Marching Band

(Marching Band Members march onstage, each holding two small American flags.)

NARRATOR: We're here to celebrate our flag today!

(Marching Band marches back and forth across stage in front of flagpole.)

MARCHING BAND: **YANKEE DOODLE FLAG**
Sung to: "Yankee Doodle"

We will march to town today
And have a celebration.
We will sing about our flag
To honor our great nation.
Yankee Doodle, keep it up,
Yankee Doodle dandy.
Our flag is such a special thing,
Let's all keep it handy.

(Marching Band Members march offstage into audience where each gives one of his or her flags to an audience member. Then Marching Band marches back onstage while singing next verse. Skip verse if no audience is present.)

We brought along some flags today
To wave for our great nation.
Here's a flag for you to wave.
Please join our celebration.
Yankee Doodle, keep it up,
Yankee Doodle dandy.
Our flag is such a special thing,
Let's all keep it handy.

(Marching Band and audience wave flags as Marching Band marches back and forth across stage.)

MARCHING BAND: **OH, WHEN THE FLAGS COME MARCHING IN**
Sung to: "When the Saints Go Marching In"

Oh, when the flags come marching in,
Oh, when the flags come marching in.
How we love to see our three colors,
When the flags come marching in.

First comes the red, then white and blue,
First comes the red, then white and blue.
How we love to see our three colors,
When the flags come marching in.

(Marching Band marches offstage and places flags in a designated spot. Each Marching Band Member then picks up a bell, a drum or a horn. Marching Band Members with bells march onstage playing instruments.)

Oh, hear the bells come marching in,
Oh, hear the bells come marching in.
We ring the bells for our great nation,
For the red and white and blue.

(Marching Band Members with drums march onstage playing instruments.)

Oh, hear the drums come marching in,
Oh, hear the drums come marching in.
We beat the drums for our great nation,
For the red and white and blue.

(Marching Band Members with horns march onstage playing instruments.)

Oh, hear the horns come marching in,
Oh, hear the horns come marching in.
We toot the horns for our great nation,
For the red and white and blue.

NARRATOR:

Let's march around the flagpole!

(Marching Band forms a circle and marches around flagpole.)

MARCHING BAND:

DOWN AT THE FLAGPOLE
Sung to: "Down by the Station"

Down at the flagpole early in morning,
We will raise our flag to honor this great land.
We will play our bells as we march around it.
Ring, ring, ring, ring goes our band.

Down at the flagpole early in morning,
We will raise our flag to honor this great land.
We will play our drums as we march around it.
Rat-a-tat, rat-a-tat goes our band.

Down at the flagpole early in morning,
We will raise our flag to honor this great land.
We will play our horns as we march around it.
Toot, toot, toot, toot goes our band.

(Marching Band lines up facing audience and marches in place.)

MARCHING BAND: **YANKEE DOODLE FLAG**
Sung to: "Yankee Doodle"

Now we've sung our songs today,
To honor our great nation.
We're so glad that we all came
And had this celebration.
Yankee Doodle, keep it up,
Yankee Doodle dandy.
Our flag is such a special thing,
Let's all keep it handy.

(Marching Band Members salute and march offstage.)

THE END

Suggested Props: Small American flags; bells; drums; horns; an American flag on a short flagpole that is tied to a chair or anchored in a bucket of rocks. Additional prop and costume suggestions for this musical can be found on p. 77.

Additional Prop
and
Costume Suggestions

On the following pages you will find prop and costume ideas that can be used in addition to those suggested at the end of each musical.

- Decide for yourself how elaborate you want your production to be. Feel free to pick and choose the prop and costume suggestions you think would work best with your children.

- Feel free also to change or to adapt any of the suggestions to fit your particular circumstances or budget.

- Whenever possible, let the children help in making the props.

- Encourage the children to come up with their own prop and costume ideas. Add your ideas as well to give the production your own special touch!

Teddy Bears' Picnic

- Make a cap with ears for each Teddy Bear. Cut two rectangles (about 2 inches by 12 inches) and two ear shapes (about 4 inches tall) out of fuzzy brown material (available at craft stores). Gather the ear shapes slightly at the bottom. Sew the long edges of the two rectangles together with the ear shapes in between so that the ears stand up from the cap. Attach ribbons to the sides of the cap to use for tying under the child's chin.

- Make a nose for each Teddy Bear. Cut a small circle out of brown construction paper. Use a black felt-tip marker to color in a nose and a mouth. Attach the circle to the child's nose with a loop of transparent tape (rolled sticky side out).

- Make a honey tree prop for the stage. Stack three large cardboard ice cream buckets on top of one another (open ends up) and tape them together to make a trunk. Glue a large circle cut from brown construction paper on the side of the top bucket to make a tree hollow. (If desired, glue a few construction paper bees around the hollow.) Cut a large treetop shape out of heavy cardboard and paint it green. Cut two slits (9½ inches apart) in the bottom edge of the shape and push the slits down over the edge of the top ice cream bucket.

Down Storybook Lane

- Make a nose for each of the Three Little Pigs. Cut a small circle out of pink construction paper. Use a black felt-tip marker to color two small circles in the center of the pink circle. Attach the pink circle to the child's nose with a loop of transparent tape (rolled sticky side out).

- Make a nose for each of the Three Bears. Cut a small circle out of brown construction paper. Use a black felt-tip marker to color in a nose and a mouth. Attach the circle to the child's nose with a loop of transparent tape.

- Make a nose for each of the Three Blind Mice. Cut a small circle out of black construction paper. Cut the circle halfway through, roll it into a cone shape and tape the edges in place. Glue on whiskers cut from black construction paper. Attach the cone shape to the child's nose with a loop of transparent tape.

- Make a nose for each of the Three Little Kittens. Cut a small circle out of gray construction paper. Glue on a nose and whiskers cut from pink construction paper. Attach the circle to the child's nose with a loop of transparent tape.

Off to Bed We Go

- Have All Characters (including Shadows, Midnight Monsters and Stars) wear pajamas.

- Make a forehead mask for each Midnight Monster. Paint a monster face on the back of a paper plate (or glue on precut facial features) and tape on horns and crepe paper "hair." Attach the mask face to a paper headband that fits around the child's forehead, making sure that the chin of the mask is above the child's eyes.

- If available, use small pocket flashlights as props for the Stars. Otherwise, cut star shapes out of construction paper circles and tape the circles over the glass ends of ordinary flashlights.

Santa's Workshop

- Make a stocking cap for each Elf. Cut a large triangle out of red or green tissue paper. With the point of the triangle at the top, fold the triangle in half lengthwise. Glue the long edges together, leaving the bottom open. Attach a cotton ball to the top of the hat and flop the top over to the side.

- Make a dancing cape for each Dancing Doll. Tape colored crepe paper strips to a long piece of yarn. Safety-pin the center of the yarn to the back of the child's collar and tie the ends together in front. (Or tie the yarn around the child's waist, if desired.)

- Make a train car prop for each Train. Cut the top and the bottom out of a large cardboard box. On opposite sides of the box, cut oblong holes near the top edges for handles. Decorate the four sides of the box to make it look like a train car. Have the child step inside the box and hold it up by the handles as he or she chugs around.

- Make a tall hat for each Toy Soldier. Tape a piece of construction paper around an oatmeal box or other round cardboard container. Glue a hat brim to the bottom edge of the box and decorate the top part of the hat as desired. Attach thick yarn to the sides of the hat to use for tying under the child's chin.

- Make a twirling cap for each Top. Make a cone-shaped hat out of construction paper and cut off the top to make a small hole. Tape crepe paper strips around the inside of the hat (near the top) and pull them out through the hole. Attach yarn to the sides of the hat to use for tying under the child's chin.

- Decorate the stage to look like Santa's workshop. Use props such as a worktable, tools, paint cans and brushes, toys, Christmas wrapping paper, ribbons, bows, etc.

Singing in the Rain

- Have the Children wear raincoats, rain hats and boots and carry small umbrellas.

- Have the Farmers wear overalls, straw hats and garden gloves and carry small garden tools.

- Make a nose for each Pig. Cut a small circle out of pink construction paper. Use a black felt-tip marker to color two small circles in the center of the pink circle. Attach the pink circle to the child's nose with a loop of transparent tape (rolled sticky side out).

- Make a bill and two feet for each Duck. Cut a duck bill shape and two webfoot shapes out of orange construction paper. Use loops of transparent tape to attach the duck bill shape to the child's nose and the webfoot shapes to the tops of the child's shoes.

Dancing Colors

• Have the Colors dress in the colors that they are representing.

• Make a dancing cape for each of the Colors. Tape appropriate colored crepe paper strips to a long piece of yarn. Safety-pin the center of the yarn to the back of the child's collar and tie the ends together in front. (Or tie the yarn around the child's waist, if desired.)

• Make a rainbow mural to use as a backdrop for the stage. Paint colored arcs from top to bottom in this order: red, orange, yellow, green, blue, purple.

In a Spring Garden

- Have the Flowers dress all in green.

- Make a flower mask for each Flower. Cut the center out of a paper plate. Turn the plate over and glue construction paper petals around the rim (or cut notches around the outside of the rim to make petals and paint the entire rim in a bright color). Attach yarn to the sides of the mask to use for tying around the child's head.

- Make a bee body for each Bee. Paint black stripes lengthwise on a long piece of yellow construction paper. Wrap the paper around the upper part of the child's body and tape the edges together in back. For wings, cut a large figure-eight shape out of waxed paper and gather it in the middle. Staple the middle of the wings shape on the back of the bee body near the top edge.

- Make a set of wings for each Bird. Tape colored crepe paper strips to a long piece of yarn. Safety-pin the center of the yarn to the back of the child's collar and tie the ends of the yarn around the child's wrists.

- Use two colorful scarves (or squares of filmy material) to make wings for each Butterfly. Have the child wear a long-sleeved shirt. Then safety-pin one edge of a scarf along each of the child's sleeves from wrist to shoulder.

Under the Big Top

- Make a clown hat for each Clown. Cut a large circle out of construction paper. Cut the circle halfway through, roll it into a cone shape to fit the child's head and tape the edges in place. Decorate the hat as desired. Attach yarn to the sides of the hat to use for tying under the child's chin.

- Make a collar for each Clown. Cut a large donut shape out of white construction paper and cut through the shape to make an opening. Place the shape over the child's shoulders and tape the ends together in back.

- Make a nose for each Clown. Cut a small circle out of red construction paper. Attach the circle to the child's nose with a loop of transparent tape (rolled sticky side out).

- Have the Dancing Bears wear dancing clothes (tights, tutus, etc.).

- Make a little hat for each Dancing Bear. Turn a medium-sized paper cup upside down and decorate it as desired with stickers, yarn, etc. Glue a cotton ball on top of the hat. Attach yarn to the sides of the hat to use for tying under the child's chin.

- Make a nose for each Dancing Bear. Cut a small circle out of brown construction paper. Use a black felt-tip marker to color in a nose and a mouth. Attach the circle to the child's nose with a loop of transparent tape.

- Make a trunk for each Elephant. Cut a long 2-inch-wide strip and a 2-inch circle out of gray construction paper. Accordion-fold the paper strip. Use a black felt-tip marker to color two small circles in the center of the gray circle and attach the gray circle to one end of the paper strip. Attach the other end of the strip to the child's nose with a loop of transparent tape.

In the Deep Blue Sea

- Make a diver's mask for each Diver. Cut a 2½-inch section out of an oatmeal box or other round cardboard container that measures 4 inches across. Cut a notch to fit over the child's nose in one edge of the section. Place a piece of clear plastic wrap over the other end and secure it with a rubber band. Cover the outside of the cardboard section with construction paper. Attach thick yarn to the sides of the mask to use for tying behind the child's head.

- Make a forehead mask for each Fish. Cut a fish shape out of colored construction paper and add details with a black felt-tip marker. Attach the fish shape to a paper headband that fits around the child's forehead, making sure that the bottom of the fish shape is above the child's eyes.

- Make a forehead mask for each Crab. Cut a crab shape out of orange construction paper and follow the directions for making the Fish mask above.

- Have the children who act the part of the Octopus all dress in the same color (gray or white, if possible).

- Make a forehead mask for each Oyster. Cut an oyster shell shape out of white construction paper and follow the directions for making the Fish mask above.

- Make an underwater mural to use as a backdrop for the stage. Paint the background blue. Then glue on sand, crepe paper "seaweed" and precut shapes of coral, fish, shells, etc.

- Throughout the performance, have the characters who are standing offstage blow bubbles out onto the stage.

Yankee Doodle Parade

- Have the Marching Band Members wear blue (or dark-colored) pants and white tops. Wrap red crepe paper streamers around their waists to make sashes.

- Make a folded paper hat for each Marching Band Member. Fold a large piece of newsprint (about 24 inches by 28 inches) in half crosswise. Then fold it in half again. With the second fold at the top, fold over the two sides of the paper so that they meet in the middle, forming a triangle. Fold up the bottom edges of the paper twice to make a hat rim and secure the edges with tape. Decorate the hat with red, silver and blue star stickers. (These hats can also be made with sheets of newspaper. Use pages that have an allover pattern, such as the classified ads pages.)

Activities, songs and new ideas to use right now are waiting for you in every issue of the TOTLINE newsletter.

Each issue puts the fun into teaching with 24 pages of challenging and creative activities for young children. All of the musicals in *Mini-Mini Musicals* first appeared in the TOTLINE.

Sample issue $1 • One year subscription $15 (6 issues)

Beautiful bulletin boards, games and flannelboards are easy with PRESCHOOL PATTERNS.

You won't want to miss a single issue of PRESCHOOL PATTERNS with 3 large sheets of patterns delightfully and simply drawn. Each issue includes patterns for making flannelboard characters, bulletin boards, learning games and more!

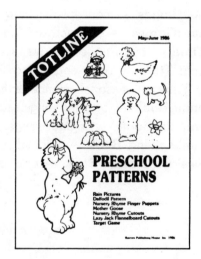

Sample issue $2 • One year subscription $18 (6 issues)

ORDER FROM:
Warren Publishing House, Inc., P.O. Box 2255, Everett, WA 98203

Also available from the Totline catalog.

Super Snacks — 120 seasonal sugarless snack recipes. 64 pg. **$3.95**
Teaching Tips — 300 helpful hints for working with young children. 64 pg. **$3.95**
Piggyback Songs — 110 original songs, sung to the tunes of childhood favorites. 64 pg. **$4.95**
More Piggyback Songs — 195 more original songs. 96 pg. **$6.95**
Piggyback Songs for Infants and Toddlers — 160 original songs for infants and toddlers. 80 pg. . . . **$6.95**
Piggyback Songs in Praise of God — 185 original religious songs. 80 pg. **$6.95**
Piggyback Songs in Praise of Jesus — 240 original religious songs. 96 pg. **$7.95**
1-2-3 Art — over 200 open-ended art activities. 160 pg. **$12.95**
1-2-3 Games — 70 no-lose games for ages 2-8. 80 pg. **$6.95**
Teeny-Tiny Folktales — 15 folktales plus flannelboard patterns. 80 pg. **$6.95**
Short-Short Stories — 18 stories plus seasonal activities. 80 pg. **$6.95**
Mini-Mini Musicals — 10 musicals, sung to familiar tunes. 80 pg. **$6.95**
"Cut & Tell" Scissor Stories for Fall — 8 original stories plus patterns. 80 pg. **$5.95**
"Cut & Tell" Scissor Stories for Winter — 8 original stories plus patterns. 80 pg. **$5.95**
"Cut & Tell" Scissor Stories for Spring — 8 original stories plus patterns. 80 pg. **$5.95**
Crafts — seasonal craft ideas. 80 pg. **$7.95**
Learning Games — concept-teaching games. 80 pg. **$7.95**
Language Games — unstructured language experiences. 80 pg. **$7.95**
Story Time — open-ended stories, songs and rhymes. 80 pg. **$7.95**
Movement Time — open-ended movement activities. 80 pg. **$7.95**
Science Time — seasonal science activities. 80 pg. **$7.95**
The Bunny Book — original songs, activities and recipes. 70 pg. **$3.95**
The Pumpkin Book — original songs, activities and recipes. 80 pg. **$3.95**
The Thanksgiving Book — original songs, activities and recipes. 80 pg. **$3.95**
The Elves' Christmas Book — original songs, activities and recipes. 72 pg. **$3.95**

★ ★ ★*Write for our FREE catalog*★ ★ ★

Warren Publishing House, Inc. • P.O. Box 2255, Dept. B • Everett, WA 98203

Send check or money order (plus 10% postage).
US funds only. WA State orders include 7.8% sales tax.